Be Quiet, Marina!

Thanks to the Bank Street Family Center
for nurturing Moira and Marina, along
with many other children. And also thanks
for letting us tell the story.

Be Quiet, Marina!

By Kirsten DeBear

Photographs by Laura Dwight

Star Bright Books
New York

Printed in China 9 8 7 6 5 4 3 2 1

Design by Design Press, a division of the Savannah College of Art and Design.

Library of Congress Cataloging-in-Publication Data

DeBear, Kirsten.
    Be quiet, Marina! / by Kirsten DeBear ; photographs by Laura Dwight.
        p. cm.
Summary: A noisy little girl with cerebral palsy and a quiet little girl
with Down syndrome learn to play together and eventually become best
friends.
    ISBN 1-887734-79-1
    [1. Friendship--Fiction. 2. Play--Fiction. 3. Cerebral palsy--Fiction.
4. Physically handicapped--Fiction. 5. Down syndrome--Fiction. 6.
Mentally handicapped--Fiction.] I. Dwight, Laura, ill. II. Title.
    PZ7.D3526 Be 2001
    [E]--dc21
                                                    00-012235

For Moira and Marina and their families.

This is Marina.   This is Moira.

 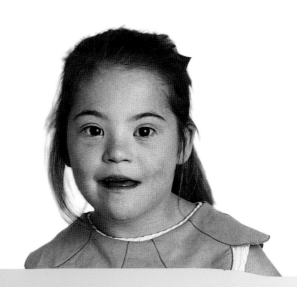

Marina and Moira go to the same
school and are good friends.

In the beginning it was hard for
them to play together. This story
will tell you why that was so, and
how they became good friends.

In many ways Marina and Moira were the same.
Marina was four years old.
Moira was also four years old.

They both liked to dance.

They both liked to
play ball.

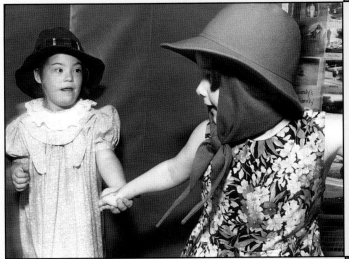

They both liked to
dress up.

And they both liked
to play with dolls.

In other ways they were different.
Marina had short hair. Moira had long hair.

Marina liked
noise. She liked
to scream and
shout.

She liked to tell Moira
what to do when they
played together.

Moira did not like noise.
She liked to sit quietly
in her cubby.

And she liked to play
with little people.

Marina liked to run ahead when the class went walking. Moira liked to stay with the teachers and other children.

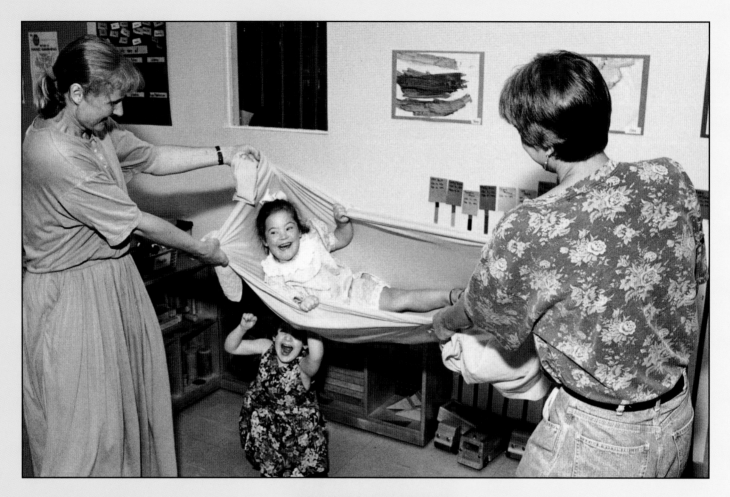

Sometimes the teachers swung the children in a blanket. Both Moira and Marina liked that.

But Marina did not like to wait for her turn. She got angry and screamed and cried.

That made
Moira feel
scared.

So she covered her
ears and went
away into the hall.

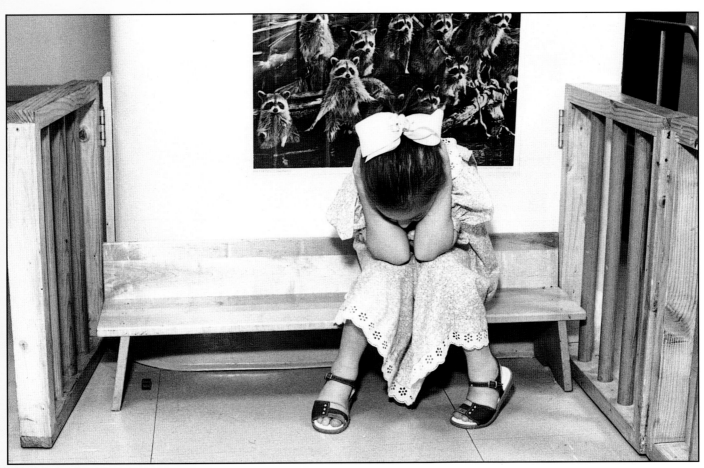

Both Marina and Moira liked to play with blocks.

When they finished they had to clean up. But Marina did not like to do that.

She got angry and screamed. Her screaming frightened Moira. So she covered her ears...

...and went away.

One day on the playground
Moira was on the see-saw.
Marina wanted to get on,
too. But she couldn't . . .

So she started
to scream.

She screamed so loudly
that Moira covered
her ears and walked
away.

Now Marina could get
on the see-saw, but it
was no fun alone.

Another day when Moira and Marina were playing telephones, Marina started to get upset.

This time something different happened. Moira did not run away. Instead she said,

"Please don't scream!"

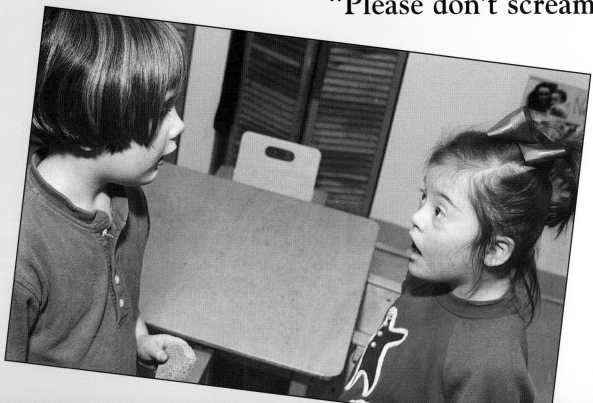

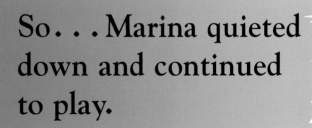

So . . . Marina quieted down and continued to play.

Another day, when Marina asked Moira, "Can I play with you?" Moira said,

"Yes, but don't scream!"

"O.K.," said Marina, "I won't."

Then they played birthday party and dolls together.

Moira used to be scared of Marina. But now she knows that Marina is her friend and she can tell her not to scream. And Marina knows that if she wants to play with Moira she must not scream.

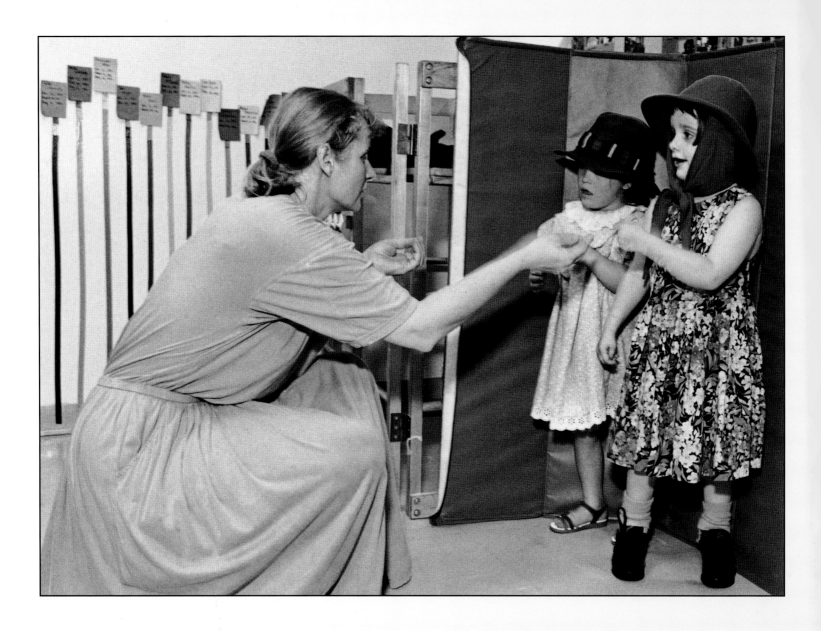

And they also know that they can
ask their teacher to help them.

Now Marina and Moira are good friends.

Marina and Moira love to play on the see-saw together. It balances and they go up and down together.

"It's fun!" screams Marina.

Moira almost lets go of the handle to cover her ears, but instead she shouts:

Be Quiet, Marina!

In many ways Marina and Moira are just like other children. Some children are loud like Marina, while others prefer quiet like Moira.

But in some ways, Marina and Moira are different from other children because of their disabilities.

Marina was born with cerebral palsy. She cannot make her right hand do what she wants. This makes it impossible for her to play with things for which she needs two hands. Her left leg is also a problem. It is hard for her to lift it or balance on it. She has to wear a brace, or 'orthotics,' inside her shoe to help her walk. She needs help to learn to balance and to use her left hand along with her right.

It is hard for Marina to take it easy. She would like to move fast and do what she wants to do without help. She gets confused and angry when her body won't do what she wants it to do.

Moira has Down syndrome. People with Down syndrome have similar facial features. Like all people with Down syndrome, Marina's fingers are shorter than those of most children her age, and she needs extra help to learn to do some things that other children find easy. It is hard for her to jump and to learn to ride a tricycle.

Marina and Moira may look and act differently because of their disabilities, but their feelings are the same as everyone else's. All of us sometimes feel that there is too much noise and we want to run away, like Moira. And all of us have times when we feel frustrated and want to scream, like Marina. We all have to learn to live in a world full of noise and commotion, and we all have to learn to tolerate frustration. Moira and Marina teach us that in spite of difficulties and differences, we can all get along.

Resources

UNITED STATES

Council for Exceptional Children
1110 N. Glebe Road, Suite 300
Arlington, VA 22201-5704
Phone: (888) CEC-SPED
Fax: (703) 264-9494
e-mail: service@cec.sped.org
http://www.cec.sped.org/index.html

National Down Syndrome Congress
7000 Peachtree-Dunwoody Road NE
Lake Ridge 400 Office Park
Building 5, Suite 100
Atlanta, GA 30328-1655
Phone: (800) 232-NDSC (770) 604-9500
mail: NDSCcenter@aol.com
http://www.ndsccenter.org

National Down Syndrome Society
666 Broadway, Suite 810
New York, NY 10012
Phone: (800) 221-4602 (212) 460-9330
Fax: (212) 979-2873
e-mail: info@ndss.org
http://www.ndss.org

**National Information Center for
Children and Youth with Disabilities**
(NICHCY)
P.O. Box 1492
Washington, DC 20013-1492
Phone: (800) 695-0285
Fax: (202) 884-8441
e-mail: nichcy@aed.org
http://www.nichcy.org

United Cerebral Palsy Association
1660 L Street NW, Suite 700
Washington, DC 20036
Phone: (800) 872-5827
Fax: (202) 776-0414
e-mail: webmaster@ucp.org
http://www.ucpa.org

CANADA

Canadian Down Syndrome Society
811 14th Street N.W.
Calgary, Alberta T2N 2A4
Phone: (800) 883-5608 (403) 270-8500
Fax: (403) 270-8291
e-mail: dsinfo@cdss.ca
http://www.cdss.ca

Cerebral Palsy Association in Alberta
#10, 8180 Macleod Trail South
Calgary, Alberta T2H 2B8
Phone: (403) 543-1161
Fax: (403) 543-1168
http://www.cerebralpalsycanada.com

Ontario Federation for Cerebral Palsy
1630 Lawrence Ave W, Ste 104
Toronto, Ontario M6L 1C5
Phone: (877) 244-9686 (416) 244-9686
Fax: (416) 244-6543
e-mail: ofcp@ofcp.on.ca
http://www.ofcp.on.ca

UNITED KINGDOM

Down Syndrome Association
155 Mitcham Road
London SW17 9PG
Phone: (020) 8682 4001
Fax: (020) 8682 4012
e-mail: info@downs-syndrome.org.uk
http://www.dsa-uk.com

SCOPE
12 Park Crescent
London W1N 4EQ
Phone: (0808) 800 3333
e-mail: cphelpline@scope.org.uk
http://www.scope.org.uk

AUSTRALIA

**Cerebral Palsy Association
of Western Australia**
106 Bradford St
Coolbinia, Western Australia 6050
Toll free: (1800) 198 263
Phone: (08) 9443 0211 Fax: (08) 9444-7299
e-mail: cpawa@iinet.net.au
http://members.iinet.net.au/~cpawa/

**Down Syndrome Association
of New South Wales, Inc.**
31 O' Connell Street
Parramatta, N.S.W. 2150
PO Box 2356
North Parramatta, N.S.W. 1750
Phone: (02) 9683 4333 Fax: (02) 9683 4020
e-mail: dsansw@hartingdale.com.au
http://www.hartingdale.com.au/~dsansw/

Down Syndrome Association of Victoria
495 High Street
Northcote, Victoria 3070
Phone: (03) 9486 2377 Fax: (03) 9486 2435
e-mail: dsavic@netspace.net.au
http://www.dsav.asn.au

SOUTH AFRICA

Down Syndrome Association
87 Waterfall Avenue
Craighall, Johannesburg 2196
Phone: (011) 788 1603
Mon-Thurs. 8:30-12:30

**Down Syndrome Association
of Kwazulu/Natal**
Box 70048
Overpoort, Durban 4067
Phone: (031) 283 882 Fax: (031) 527 486